Carole Bosanko worked as a clinical psychologist in the National Health Service for over 30 years. She is also a mindful self-compassion teacher and has run many courses, workshops and events across the UK.

Carole uses meditation, mindfulness and self-compassion within her own life and is passionate about developing approaches that help people improve their health and well-being.

This is the first of a series of books that show how mindfulness and self-compassion can enhance our daily lives.

To Matt and Beckie and their cats, Annabelle and Phoebe.

Carole Bosanko

MINDFULNESS FOR CAT LOVERS

AUSTIN MACAULEY PUBLISHERS™

LONDON • CAMBRIDGE • NEW YORK • SHARJAH

A CIP catalogue record for this title is available from the British Library.

ISBN 9781528926102 (Paperback)
ISBN 9781528932806 (Hardback)
ISBN 9781528933032 (ePub e-book)

www.austinmacauley.com

First Published (2021)
Austin Macauley Publishers Ltd
25 Canada Square
Canary Wharf
London
E14 5LQ

Acknowledgements

Firstly, special thanks to my family, particularly to mum and dad who taught me through their 'being'; love, compassion and kindness. To my husband, Alex, for his generosity of spirit and unswerving love. To my son, Matt, and daughter-in-law, Beckie, for being the great people they are and for shining a light on their special relationship with their cats, Annabelle and Phoebe. Also to Matt for his thoughts and guidance at the earlier stages of this book.

My thanks to Geraldine Crawford for her informal editorial input; the feedback she provided was always clear and creative, laughter was shared and a friendship was deepened. My love and thanks also go to Sue Wilson for her belief in this book and her eye for detail in the early 'proofreading'; this is a friendship deeply treasured. Thanks also to my dear friend, Jacquie Blakeley, who was an early supporter of this book. Her enthusiasm, humour and ongoing open-door policy to all things feline (and also other animals!) are always greatly valued. Each of you have enriched my life.

Gratitude and love to my friends who enthusiastically sent photographs of their cats: Elaine Gordon with William G, Geraldine Crawford with Boo and Poussey, Ray Dennis with Tux, Jane McGill-Hoyland with William and Georgie, Julie Hammersley with Cookie, Kate Downing with Poppy, Pru Madeley with Cecilia and Toby and Linda Thomas with Jack.

A big thank you also to all my other friends; whilst our family gives us roots, our friends give us wings…thanks to you all for helping me 'fly'.

Great respect and thanks also goes to Dr Kristin Neff and Dr Chris Germer for the wonderful training they provided on mindful self-compassion and for the great work they do in trying to make people's worlds, and the wider world, kinder and more compassionate places.

Finally, many thanks go to the Austin Macauley team for believing in this book.

Table of Contents

"I have lived with several Zen Masters; all of them cats."
– Eckhart Tolle

Introduction

As a clinical psychologist working within the National Health Service for over 30 years, I helped people from all backgrounds and with a range of complex needs. Increasingly, I began to recognise that simple wellbeing techniques practised regularly, helped many of my clients. I developed and began to offer psycho-educational courses which included relaxation and mindfulness exercises.

I love the simplicity yet powerfulness of mindfulness, and with retirement came the space to look at new ways of sharing my knowledge and my enthusiasm. I know first-hand how powerful mindfulness and relaxation can be.

I want to make mindfulness more easily accessible…to find a way that invites people to find out a bit more, in a way that is fun, in a way that naturally fits with things they love and already have in their lives and maybe even in a way that simply shines a light on what they might already be mindfully doing without realising it!

This book is designed as a taster, to be light, helpful, entertaining and it might even be your start on the path of a wonderful mindful journey…

"There are two means of rescue from the miseries of life: Music and Cats."
– Albert Schweitzer

"There are three means of rescue from the miseries of life: Music, Cats and Mindfulness!"
– Carole Bosanko

Mindfulness Practices

Mindfulness means being aware of the present moment with acceptance. Mindfulness makes us more aware of what is happening in our bodies (i.e. physical sensations and feelings), our minds (i.e. thoughts and the stories we tell ourselves about how things are) and in our surroundings. Many of us operate on autopilot, being 'mindless' of many things...with this we miss out on the fullness and richness of life and ourselves.

Mindfulness can help reduce stress, manage ill health, help depression, improve sleep, boost the immune system and make life feel better.

As a mindful self-compassion teacher, how is it that I've written a book about mindfulness and cats?! The mindfulness bit makes sense but what about the cats?

It's simple! Cats have many mindfulness qualities and already bring them into our lives. Having a cat can trigger the release of calming chemicals which can lower stress and anxiety levels. As cats live in the present moment and have a soothing influence, they make the perfect pet to demonstrate the principles and benefits of mindfulness. Cats can make it easy to be mindful.

Cats bring smiles, warmth, affection and laughter. They make us feel good when curled up on our laps. Even their purring can provide calmness and relaxation.

Cats can also be confidants and companions. They can be told troubles and they just sit there and purr...no judgement, just listening.

So cats bring warmth, humour and companionship. They know us, respond to us and just make us feel better!

And so, this book was born...

How to Get the Most from this Book

The following simple mindfulness and self-compassion exercises will help you find peace in your day and build happiness and gratitude into your life. They take very little effort, not much time and can generally be done anywhere, at any time. Most are with your cat (more pleasant) but some are done on your own.

This book will give you 'cat exercises' that will show you how to be more like your cat (that is in their mindfulness!), and also how to use your cat to create more mindfulness and self-compassion in your day.

The book is not meant to be worked through systematically; you can dip into it as you have the time. Also, when needed for the exercise, when your cat is with you!

It is divided into four sections: 'Mindfulness and Relaxation', 'Gratitude, Appreciation and Happiness', 'Self-Care and Self-Compassion', 'Cats and Resilience'. Each section has, within it, exercises that are short (up to five minutes), medium (5–10 minutes) and long (10–20 minutes), so you can choose what you want to do and for how long.

Some general ideas for getting the most from the book are:

- Read through each exercise slowly before you do it.
- Prepare what you need for the exercise.
- Make sure you are warm enough.
- Make sure the chair, floor or bed is comfy.
- If you are uncomfortable at any time during the exercise, just move to make yourself

comfortable…this is not about having to stay perfectly still.

- Make sure you're not going to be interrupted by people, phones or animals…unless it is your cat and you need her / him for the exercise!
- Thoughts will come into your head. This is perfectly normal, so just try to treat them as if they were clouds. Observe them, then let them drift by…there's no need to try to push them, pull them or force them along. Just let them pass.
- Treat any distractions as if they are thoughts and as you become aware that you have drifted away from the exercise, come back to it and recommence.
- If at any time it becomes too difficult or uncomfortable, then stop the exercise.

SO, LET'S GET STARTED…

Mindfulness and Relaxation

"What greater gift than the love of a cat?"
– Charles Dickens

Mindful 'Cat Observing'

Focusing on a single object helps to bring your mind to the present moment. Whilst you are focusing and noticing everything about it, you are not putting time and attention into worrying about other parts of your life.

This exercise is about observing every detail of your cat. A good way to start this, is to look at your cat, as if for the first time.

Duration: 5–10 minutes **(Medium)**.
What this is good for: This is the perfect exercise to start practicing mindfulness as it encourages increased awareness and being in the present moment.
What you need: A cat on your lap!
Exercise:

- Feel the way your cat settles into your lap.
- Notice the contours of your cat's body; be aware of its shape.
- As it sits on your lap, notice; is the warmth all over your lap or is there a warm spot?
- As you stroke your cat from head to tail, observe how your cat responds.
- Notice any change in the feeling of the fur.
- Look at your cat's eyes; what shape, colour and shades are they? Are there flecks?

- Listen to your cat breathing, and see if you can slow your own breathing to mirror it.
- When your cat gets up to leave, just recognise her /his independent spirit and let them go.

This is Poppy and she sleeps all day long.

"Like a graceful vase, a cat, even when motionless, seems to flow."

– George F. Will

Mindful 'Cat Listening'

Sound is one of our five senses that can quickly get enmeshed with associated meaning and memories. So learning to just listen, without labelling or judging, is a good way to start mindful listening.

Duration: 1–5 minutes **(Short)**.
What this is good for: Learning to listen and not label or judge.
What you need: A cat and your listening skills.
Exercise:

- Thoroughly immerse yourself in the sounds of your cat.
- Be aware of it purring. Listen to the purring and see if you can feel the vibrations from it in your body.
- Be aware of your cat padding,
- Be aware of her/him breathing.
- Then just see if you can mirror your cat's breath. Try to slow your breathing down to synchronise with your cat.
- Be aware of any other sounds your cat is making.
- Be aware of any surrounding silence.
- As the exercise finishes, just take a few slow, deep breaths.

This is Phoebe…'Purring' is her speciality.

"A meow massages the heart."
– Stuart McMillan

Mindful 'Cat Seeing'

This exercise is about seeing things through the eyes of your cat.

Duration: 5–10 minutes **(Medium)**.
What this is good for: Really looking, seeing and not judging…the basics of mindfulness.
What you need: A cat and a window with a view.
Exercise:

- Find a space at the window near your cat.
- Look at everything your cat is looking at; then look more closely.
- Try to avoid labelling what you see; instead of thinking 'car', 'bird', 'fly', 'bee' or 'trees', try to notice the colours and the patterns.
- Pay attention to the movement and notice the many different shapes. Try to see these things as if seeing them for the first time.
- If your mind wanders and you become distracted, gently bring your mind back and notice the colours, patterns or movement again, to put you back in the present moment.
- Be observant, but not critical. Be aware, but not fixated.
- As the exercise ends, take a few slow, deep breaths, in through your nose and out through your mouth.

Poppy just loves looking out of the window.

"Prowling his own quiet backyard or asleep by the fire, he is still only a whisker away from the wilds."
– Jean Burden

Mindful 'Cat Five Senses'

'Cat Five Senses' can help you to quickly bring awareness to the present moment. It is about noticing something that your cat is experiencing with each of the five senses.

Duration: 5–10 minutes **(Medium).**
What this is good for: Quickly becoming mindful in most situations.
What you need: Something your cat is experiencing.
Exercise:

- Notice five things that your cat can **see**. Look around you and bring your attention to five things that can be seen. Pick things that you don't normally notice.
- Notice four things that your cat can **feel**. Bring your awareness to four things like the feeling of the breeze, the temperature of the floor surface or the texture of a cushion.
- Notice three things your cat can **hear**. Take a moment to listen, and note three things that you hear in the background. For example, this might be the chirp of a bird, the hum of a bee or the sound of traffic.
- Notice two things your cat can **smell**. Bring your awareness to all smells whether they're pleasant or unpleasant.
- Notice one thing you can **taste**. Focus on one thing that you can taste right now. For this you can drink or eat something, or just notice the taste in your mouth.
- Then finish by taking a few slow, deep breaths.

This is Cookie absorbed in 'the moment' of the flowers.

"I take care of my flowers and my cats, enjoy food and that's living."

– Ursula Andress

Mindful 'Cat Breathing'

This exercise is about being still and focussing on your cat's breath for at least one minute! The breath is a core exercise with mindfulness as it is always there. It helps you to bring your attention out of your head and into your body, and in turn has a calming effect.

Duration: 1–5 minutes **(Short)**.
What this is good for: Calming and relaxing. It creates an anchor and safe place to go to when you might be feeling wobbly or you just want a quiet moment.
What you need: A cat, a comfy chair, a clock / watch or a phone with a timer or an alarm.
Exercise:

- Set the timer for a minute or your chosen time.
- Start by carefully observing your cat breathing.
- Then begin by breathing in and out slowly for a count of three or four, trying to mirror the slow breathing of your cat.
- Fully absorb yourself in how your cat is breathing.
- Breathe in through your nose and out through your mouth, letting your breath flow effortlessly in and out.
- Try to let go of your thoughts; treat them like clouds in the sky...not pushing them or pulling them, just watching them drift by.
- Now focus on your breath and become aware of where you feel it most easily in your body; maybe your nostrils, your chest or abdomen or maybe in your whole body.
- Be aware of both the in-breath and the out-breath.
- Then come back to observing your cat breathing.
- As the timer rings, slowly come back to the sounds of the room and then to any sounds from outside.

This is Toby (affectionately known as Tobes), 'Just Chilling'.

"Time spent with cats is never wasted."
– Sigmund Freud

Mindful 'Cat Relaxation and Body Scan Meditation'

"Kittens are born with their eyes shut. They open them in about six days; take a look around and then close them again for the better part of their lives."

– Stephen Baker

Studies have shown that meditation and relaxation are good for you, reducing stress and anxiety, lifting mood, increasing alertness and heightening creativity. So, if you don't usually make time for some relaxation or meditation in your day, why not try curling up next to your cat and giving yourself a 15-minute relaxation or meditation break?

The following 'Body Scan' meditation is a good and easy way to begin.

Duration: 10–20 minutes **(Long)**.
What this is good for: Increasing awareness of bodily sensations, feelings and experiences. Letting us know what is 'normal' and what is not, so we can then try to adjust things as we need to. It is also good for calming.
What you need: A comfy chair or floor space with a mat and a sleeping cat.
Exercise:

- Begin by looking at your sleeping cat and noticing its posture, quietness and contentment.
- Observe its slow, gentle breathing.
- Then close your eyes or lower your gaze.
- Bring your awareness to your breath, noticing the rhythm and the experience of breathing in and breathing out. Then begin by breathing in and out slowly for a count of three or four, maybe even trying to mirror the slow breath of your cat.
- Now become aware of your body as a whole, how it feels, the texture of clothing against the skin and the surface on which your body is resting.

- Become aware of any sensations in your body-maybe tingling, hot or cold, heavy or light or something else.
- Also just notice any areas of your body where you don't feel any sensations at all or that are hypersensitive.
- Now just move through each part of your body in turn, paying special attention to the way each area feels: Start with both your feet and toes, then move to:
- The rest of your feet (tops, bottoms, ankles),
- Lower legs, knees and thighs,
- Bottom and pelvis,
- Abdomen,
- Lower Back,
- Upper Back,
- Chest,
- Hands (fingers, palms, backs, wrists),
- Arms (lower arms, elbows, upper arms),
- Neck, Face and Head (jaw, mouth, nose, cheeks, ears, eyes, forehead, scalp and finally the top of your head).
- Then, when you are ready, come back to the sounds of the room and the sounds of outside and gently open your eyes.
- Take a moment to observe your sleeping cat again, if he/she has not wandered off!

This is Cecilia having her afternoon nap.

"You cannot look at a sleeping cat and feel tense."
– Jane Pauley

Mindful 'Cat Walking – Paw by Paw'

This is a good way to anchor your awareness in the present moment, noticing body sensations.

Duration: 5–10 minutes **(Medium)**.
What this is good for: Body awareness. It encourages getting out of your head and into your body. It is particularly good if you want to calm yourself before an important event such as an interview, a meeting or just when you're upset.
What you need: Your cat, your feet and some floor space.
Exercise:

- First observe how your cat walks slowly and stealthily.
- Then take a few moments copying their slow, steady movement.
- Become fully aware of how you are moving; be aware of how your whole body moves, breaking it down into the smaller parts that make up the movement.
- Drop your awareness into your feet and be aware of any general sensations there.
- Notice the specific sensation of lifting your feet, then placing them on the floor.
- Now, slowly come to a standing position and just be fully aware of the bottoms of your feet.
- Now, move your feet from side to side and be aware of how this feels.
- If your mind wanders (which is normal), just feel the soles of your feet again and bring your awareness back to your body and back to your feet. And, then move them back and forward and notice where they touch the floor.
- When you are ready, expand your awareness to the whole of your body and then to your cat…if they are still in the room with you![1]

---

[1] Adapted from Singh et al, 2003

This is Jack enjoying quiet moments in his garden.

"One cat just leads to another."
– Ernest Hemingway

The Two Big Cats' Story

This story gives a message about mindfulness.

Duration: 5–10 minutes **(Medium)** and then hopefully, the rest of your life.

What this is good for: Understanding that what we focus on in our minds can get bigger!

What you need: A comfy chair and then time to read the story, absorb it and reflect on it.

Exercise:

Read the story to yourself and just take a few moments to think about its meaning and how it might be pertinent to your own life.

An old Maasai chief was teaching his granddaughter and grandson about life.

"A fight is going on inside me," he told the young children, "a fight between two big cats.

"One is evil, full of anger, sorrow, regret, greed, self-pity and false pride.

"The other is good, full of joy, peace, love, humility, kindness and faith.

"This same fight is going on inside of you, grandchildren…and inside every other person on the face of this earth."

The grandchildren ponder this for a moment and then ask, "Grandfather, which big cat will win?"

The old man smiled and simply said, "The one you feed."

So…don't deny, hurt, or try to kill the angry big cat, as you'll get into a long battle with it and it will become more powerful through the hostility and will suck life from you.

Calmly, pay attention to it, maybe thank it for trying to help you, protect you…that way it will end up lying down next to you; no longer an enemy.

The peaceful big cat will grow and become your guide through all experiences and difficulties in life.

With Mindfulness, we can choose what we bring into action and what we let go; it just takes practice.[2]

This is Archie with his friend.

"I have studied many philosophers and cats. The wisdom of cats is infinitely superior."

– Hippolite Taine

---

[2] Adapted from 'The Two Wolves'

Mindful 'Cat Colouring'

Mindful colouring is great for calming the mind and for relaxation.

Duration: 5–10 minutes or 10–20 minutes **(Medium and Long)**.

What this is good for: Reducing stress and anxiety, increasing mindfulness and creativity!

What you need: Pencil, pen, crayons, paints, rubber and paper.

Exercise:

- Mindfully colour in the cat. Immerse yourself in the moment, taking time to enjoy the activity and the calmness it can create.

"Two things are aesthetically perfect in the world – the clock and the cat."

– Emile Auguste Chartier

Mindful 'Cat Drawing'

Like mindful colouring, mindful drawing can create a sense of relaxation and calm the mind.

Duration: 5–10 minutes or 10–20 minutes **(Medium and Long)**.
What this is good for: Reducing stress and anxiety, increasing mindfulness and creativity.
What you need: Pencil, pen, crayons, paints, rubber, paper and a cat or a picture of a cat.
Exercise:

- Use your cat as a model or use a picture of a cat. Start to draw the outline.
- Really look at your cat or the picture as if you are seeing them for the first time, noticing every detail.
- Then slowly fill in the details.
- This is not about creating a masterpiece but about using the time to be fully present in the moment of drawing and to be with your cat.

This is Annie, she is just so cute.

"The smallest feline is a masterpiece."
– Leonardo da Vinci

Mindful 'Cat Writing'

Like drawing, writing can also settle the mind and become an anchor for mindfulness. By focusing on the full detail of what is seen and/or experienced, you can be fully aware in that moment.

Duration: 10–20 minutes **(Long)**.
What this is good for: Reducing stress and anxiety, increasing mindfulness and creativity.
What you need: Pen, paper or notepad and a cat or an idea about a cat.
Exercise:

- Bring your awareness to your breath, noticing the rhythm and the experience of breathing in and breathing out. Then begin by breathing slowly for a count of three or four.
- Take a few moments to settle your body and mind.
- Look around where you are and give your full attention to what your cat is doing or if your cat is not around, something else.
- Pay attention to any movement, notice the colours and the different shapes. Try to see these things as if seeing them for the first time.
- If your mind wanders and you become distracted, gently bring your mind back and notice the colours, patterns or movement again to put you back in the present moment.
- Then, write down a few lines about what you have observed.
- Take a few deep breaths, then look again; focus on all details and also maybe how it makes you feel.
- Then again, write down a few lines about what you have observed.
- End the exercise by slowly reading through what you have written.

Poppy reading her manuscript.

"If you want to write, keep cats."
– Aldous Huxley

'Compassionate Cat Friend' Meditation

In the following meditation, you are asked to imagine a cat who is a compassionate friend. This might be your cat, another cat, a cat from a story or a poem or even an imaginary cat.

Start by either reading, recording or getting a friend to read out the section marked, '**Read before doing the meditation**'. Once you have completed the meditation, then read the section, '**Read after the meditation**'.

Duration: 10–20 minutes (**Long**) but can be shortened if need be.

What this is good for: Improving mood, reducing stress and a better quality of life.

What you need: A comfy chair or floor space with a mat and your imagination.

Exercise: Read before doing the meditation

- Make yourself comfortable, either sitting or lying down.
- Then gently close your eyes.
- Take a few deep breaths to settle into your body. Now try to imagine yourself in a place that is safe and comfortable—it might be a cosy room, a garden or patio, park or a wood. It can also be an imaginary place...anywhere that feels peaceful and safe.
- Take a few moments to enjoy the feeling of comfort in this place.
- Soon you'll receive a visitor, a warm and compassionate presence—a compassionate friend that is a cat—one that embodies the qualities of wisdom and love.
- Imagine your chosen cat in as much detail as possible; especially how it feels to be with it.
- You can choose whether to go out to your cat or invite it in, or perhaps as cats do, your 'compassionate cat' will make the decision for you!

- Just be aware of how it feels to be in the company of this cat. There is nothing you need to do except to experience the moment.
- Now allow yourself to recall a moderate difficulty (about a four or five on a scale of 0-10, with ten being the most difficult) that you have in your life right now.
- Your compassionate cat friend is very wise and would like to tell you something; something that is just what you need to hear.
- Please take a moment and listen carefully to what they have come to say.
- If no words come, that's okay—just experience the loveliness of the company of your compassionate cat.
- Maybe you would like to say something to your compassionate cat. It sits quietly but listens deeply, and completely understands you. Is there anything you'd like to share?
- Soon your cat will be leaving again, but it would like to leave you with a gift—a material object. This object can either simply appear in your hands, or you can put your hands out to receive it. It is something that has special meaning to you.
- Take a few moments to look at it…What is it and what is its meaning?
- Now, enjoy your cat's presence for a few last moments, offering thanks for the visit, and then say goodbye.
- You are alone again in your safe place.
- Let yourself savour what just happened, perhaps, taking a moment to think about the words or the gift you were given.
- Now let go of the meditation and focus on your body as a whole. Allow yourself to feel whatever you feel; to be exactly as you are in this moment.
- Then gently open your eyes.

Read After the Meditation

- Your compassionate cat friend is a part of you. The presence you feel, the words you hear and the gift you receive are a deep part of your inner self. Compassion and wisdom are always available, especially when you need them the most. You can invite your compassionate cat friend back anytime you wish.[3]

This is William G and he is 'Just William'.

"Cats are connoisseurs of comfort."
– James Herriot

---

[3] Adapted from Paul Gilbert, 2009

Gratitude, Appreciation and Happiness

"Cats have it all—admiration, an endless sleep, and company only when they want it."
– Rod McKuen

Cultivating an 'attitude of gratitude' is good for you. Cats bring happiness and an opportunity for appreciation and gratitude.

We are hardwired to focus on problems and difficulties, so we often miss the opportunity to see the good things in our lives. Rick Hanson (neuropsychologist) describes this as being Teflon coated for the good and Velcro coated for the bad! By actively thinking about the good in our lives, we can balance things out and in turn create more contentment.

The following exercises encourage you to focus on all that you have, rather than concentrate on the difficulties or what you don't have. They are all about gratitude, appreciation and happiness…so you are in for a treat!

Mindful 'Cat Appreciation'

This exercise is about appreciating your cat and how it supports you in your life. Sometimes this might get overlooked in the busyness of life.

Duration: 5–10 minutes **(Medium).**
What this is good for: Improving physical, psychological health, sleep, self-esteem, empathy and resilience.
What you need: A notepad, a pen, your cat and your awareness.

Exercise:

- Simply appreciate the 'small' things that your cat brings to your life.
- Over the course of the day, notice five things about your cat that usually go unappreciated.
- List them on your notepad.
- Look at the list before you go to bed and as you wake in the morning, say each one slowly with warmth and appreciation.
- Maybe say 'Thank You 'to your cat after each one.

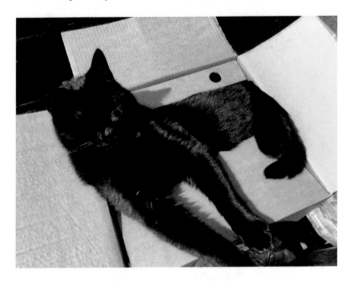

This is William with his funny ways...'The catnip has arrived. I will keep it warm until it hatches'.

"There are few things in life more heart-warming than to be welcomed by a cat."

– Tay Hohoff

Mindful 'Cat 5:3:2 for Happiness'

"One small cat changes coming home to an empty house to coming home."

– Pam Brown

'Cat 5:3:2 for Happiness' is a lovely way of starting the day with gratitude and it promotes a positive approach to the cats and people in your life.

Duration: five minutes **(Short).**
What this is good for: Training your mind to create happiness.
What you need: The time and your thoughts.
Exercise:

- Encourage your first thoughts in the morning to be about five people you are grateful to have in your life and/or five things about your cat you are grateful for.
- Then for the first three minutes, you meet your cat and/or your family; meet them like 'long lost friends'.
- Finally, think of two things you appreciate about your cat. [4]

---

[4] Adapted from 5:3:2 Technique for Happiness by Amit Sood

Phoebe – She brings joy and happiness wherever she goes.

"If we treated everyone we meet with the same affection we bestow upon our favourite cat, they, too, would purr."
– Martin Buxbaum

Mindful 'Cat Awareness and Appreciation'

This exercise is simple but powerful, as it brings an awareness and appreciation of everyday, natural elements. It allows for a connection or re-connection with the beauty of nature and the wider natural environment. These are things that are easily available but often get missed because of our busy lives.

Duration: Up to five minutes **(Short)**.

What this is good for: Appreciation of everyday things, which in turn brings you in to the present moment. It also helps increase happiness.

What you need: An object that your cat is observing, for example a bird, a leaf, a stone, a bee, a fly or a flower.

Exercise:

- Simply notice this object for a minute or two.
- Look at it as if you are seeing it through the eyes of your cat.
- Visually explore every aspect of it, the colours, the form, and the way the light plays on it. Be aware of and appreciate its beauty.
- Allow yourself to enjoy the sight of it. To fully appreciate it.
- Notice how it moves and fully absorb yourself in any movement you observe.
- Allow yourself to experience it with as many senses as possible. So, if you can, close your eyes and explore it with your sense of sound, smell, touch...
- Notice that when you are focused on your object, with appreciation, there is little room for regret or worry, for the past or the future. You are in the present moment.
- After a few minutes, become aware again of your surroundings, settle in your body and take a few slow, deep breaths.

This is Poussey and she is so inquisitive.

"By associating with the cat, one only risks becoming richer."

— **Colette**

Mindful 'Cat Activities'

This exercise is designed to cultivate an awareness and appreciation of everyday cat-related tasks, for example brushing your cat, stroking it, playing with it or feeding it.

Duration: 5–10 minutes **(Medium)**.
What this is good for: Cultivating good feelings, happiness and wellbeing.
What you need: An activity you do with your cat.
Exercise:

- Choose one activity.
- Immerse yourself in the experience, sensing it and savouring it to the fullest. Use all your senses.
- When you notice that your mind has wandered, just return to the sensations and appreciation again and again.
- So, for example, when playing with your cat:
  - Take a moment to just enjoy your cat whatever it is doing.
  - Now, start to play with her/him.
  - Notice how it feels when you immerse yourself in the moment of playing.
  - Notice how your cat responds to the playing and how you then in turn, feel.
  - Fully absorb yourself in this activity, savouring, enjoying and appreciating your cat.

Georgie with her Christmas 'Hair Do'.

**"I regard cats as one of the great joys in the world. I see
them as a gift of highest order."**
– Trisha McCagh

Self-Care and Self-Compassion

"Of all animals, he alone attains to the contemplative life."

— Andrew Lang

Self-compassion includes self-care and most of us already have a range of activities we do that are self-caring and self-nourishing. These can be routinely weaved into our lives and are especially good to put in when we are going through tougher times.

Mindful Self-Care

Duration: Up to five minutes **(Short)** for the list. Then 10–20 minutes, or longer, for the activities **(Long)**.
What this is good for: Improving health, relationships, emotional resilience and general well-being. Self-compassion is also good for reducing anxiety and depression.
What you need: Pen or pencil.
Exercise: Look at the following list of everyday ways of bringing self-care into your life and tick those you already do.

At the end, add any others you do that are not listed.

- Soak in a bath
- Read a favourite book
- Listen to music
- Look at happy photos
- Go for a walk or run
- Watch a favourite film

- Meditate for five minutes
- Write a poem
- Keep a 'Gratitude' journal
- Do a random act of kindness
- Try a Yoga, Pilates or Tai Chi class
- Have a massage, reflexology session or facial
- Make a list of things that you are thankful for
- Try a new recipe
- Have a short sleep
- Enjoy a small snack
- Have a cup of tea
- Join a new class
- Meet up with a friend
- Others, **please add**

The following is a list of everyday cat-related ways to bring self-kindness and self-care into your life. Take a look and tick those you already do and add any others at the end.

- Watch your cat at play or asleep
- Read a favourite book about cats or poems about cats
- Look at photos of your cat
- Watch videos about cats
- Meditate for five minutes with your cat
- Write a poem about cats
- Keep a 'Gratitude' journal of all the things you are grateful for about your cat
- Do a random act of kindness for your cat
- Stroke your cat
- Make a list of things that you are thankful for about your cat
- Have a short sleep with or without your cat
- Meet up with a friend at a Cat Café
- Try to be with 'Radiators' like your cat (i.e. people who give warmth and add to your life) and not 'Drains' (people who drain you and have a negative influence on your life)

- Make a list of things you can look forward to doing with your cat
- Do some of the 'Mindful Cat Lovers' exercises
- Others, **please add**

Try doing these cat and non-cat-related activities regularly (daily or weekly) and put more into your life when things are difficult.

Cecilia with her teddy bear.

"Cats do not have to be shown how to have a good time, for they are unfailing ingenious in that respect."

– James Mason

Mindful 'Cat Soothing Touch'

This is an easy and effective way to be kind to yourself. Simply giving yourself a gentle hug, putting your hand on your heart or stroking your cat can have positive physiological effects. Research indicates that safe physical touch releases oxytocin, provides a sense of security, soothes distress and calms…so it's definitely worth a try.

Duration: 5–10 minutes **(Medium)**. Then, as long as needed when going through a tough time **(Long)**.
What this is good for: Reducing anxiety, stress and increasing a sense of calm.
What you need: Your hands and your cat.
Exercise:

- Start by gently placing your hand over your heart or giving yourself a hug.
- Take 2–3 slow, deep breaths maybe, using the 'Cat Breathing' exercise.
- Become aware of your breathing, focus for a few moments on the 'in' breath and what you notice. Now switch to the 'out' breath and focus on what you notice.
- Just stay with these feelings for a short while.
- Now with your cat, start gently stroking him/her and become fully aware of the warmth of their body; the silkiness of their fur and their gentle purring.
- Fully absorb yourself in the stroking.
- Then, as the exercise ends, just take a few slow, deep breaths.

You may wish to try doing this exercise during difficult times. Simply place your hand over your heart, give yourself a hug or stroke your cat as many times in the day as you need to and then for as many days as are needed.

Toby just loves to be stroked.

**"People who love cats have some of the biggest hearts
around."**

– Susan Easterly

Cats and Resilience

"Cats know how to obtain food without labour, shelter without confinement, and love without penalties."

−   **W. L. George**

No matter how many times they fall, cats always find the will to get up and try again. They have a resilient spirit. They probably know better than we do, that just because you make a few mistakes, it doesn't mean you are forever incapable of success or doomed to failure. They have those nine lives for a reason!

With cats, this resilience is often about perseverance and trying new ways…just think of the number of different ways cats try to catch a piece of dangling string or chase a ball across the floor.

How humans and cats can cope with difficulties

Humans	Cats
Keeping a positive emotion	Purring/playing
Resilience-how we see and react to stressors	Keep on trying to catch the toy mouse
Empathy and generosity	Sensing moods and rubbing their head against you
Mindfulness	Grooming

With mindfulness, you can choose how to respond to life and its stressors. The following exercise is a great way of using mindfulness, self-compassion and building resilience. As well as these skills, it's also good to remember that FAIL means First Attempt at Learning!

'Paws' for Thought

Often, when life is difficult, we can be overly critical and hard on ourselves, but self-kindness and compassion, not criticism can bring greater resiliency and strength into our lives.

This is a helpful exercise to bring yourself compassion. It is also a great way to practice mindfulness by bringing awareness to emotions and staying in the moment with them. Simply encouraging yourself to pause (paws), can make a big difference.

Duration: 10–20 minutes **(Long)**.
What this is good for: Being kind to yourself when you are having a tough time. Choosing how you respond, increasing self-compassion and building resilience.
What you need: Your hands, your awareness and your cat if they are around.
Exercise:

- If your cat is present, just take a few moments to stroke her/him.
- Gently close your eyes.
- Start by noticing your feelings; take a moment to try to pause your thoughts and your actions. Focus on any feelings in your body.
- Scan your body from head to toe noticing any areas of tension.
- Move your hand over your heart, give yourself a hug or stroke your cat and take a few deep breaths.
- If at any time, it becomes too difficult or uncomfortable then either just stop the exercise or come back to the awareness of your breath.

- Just notice your breath rising and falling, maybe even inclining towards your own breathing in the same way you might incline towards a cat or a kitten, just noticing how they breathe.
- Then try adding a phrase that you feel offers self-kindness/compassion such as: "May I be kind to myself."
- Bring your awareness back to your breath, notice the rhythm and the experience of breathing in and breathing out. Then, begin by breathing in and out slowly for a count of three or four, maybe even trying to mirror the slow breath of your cat.
- To find out what you need, you can also ask yourself the following questions:
- What do I need right now?
- What do I **really** need?
- Maybe think about doing some of those self-care, cat-related or other activities from the earlier 'Self-Care and Self-Compassion' section.
- Now let go of this exercise and focus on your body as a whole. Allow yourself to be exactly as you are in this moment.
- Then gently open your eyes.[5]

---

[5] Adapted from Kristin Neff's Self-Compassion Break.

Georgie always knows what she needs.

"A cat has absolute emotional honesty; human beings, for one reason or another, may hide their feelings, but a cat does not."

– Ernest Hemingway

Final Word – From
a Friend and their Owner!

Summing up the beautiful relationship between cats, their owners and the mindfulness qualities, my good friend Geraldine wrote:

"We all have inner worlds. With whom we share these thoughts, may change throughout our lives. Partners, children, friends come and go. We live with others and sometimes alone. Those of us who live with cats have a special sort of experience. We share our space with them from the moment we emerge from sleep. They jump on our beds, enter our rooms appearing from nowhere, sit on our chairs, and walk on our laptops. We hear the gentle thud of the cat flap and we know instinctively whether they are in or out. They watch us and we watch them. We know their routines and they know ours. We stare at them in our gardens, stalking real or imaginary prey. We invent stories around their encounters with other visiting cats. We see them as they wash and preen themselves methodically and with such intent. We marvel at their ability to jump great heights onto our kitchen tops when we are preparing food and then land so elegantly on their feet when we shoo them away. We attribute personalities and characteristics to them. They become companions. Cats inhabit our inner worlds and mindfulness is about exploring and observing these worlds. It follows that our cats, as well as being our companions, can be our teachers to live more mindfully."

This is Boo and he often goes missing for two days at a time.

"Boo is like a teenage boy. Treats my house like a hotel—don't see him for days at a time; always hungry, a bit smelly and leaves wet paw prints everywhere. But when he snuggles up and asks for a fuss and wants his tummy tickled, all is forgiven."

– Geraldine Crawford

Following On...

If you have enjoyed doing these exercises and want to continue, you can simply repeat them whenever you want to and also make them longer. You can use the ideas of mindfulness any time and with any interaction with your cat...so maybe next time you get the 'early morning wakeup call', try turning it into a mindful moment.

If you want to read more, try out new exercises or join a course; the following information might be of interest:

Websites – Mindful Self-Compassion

- **Mindful Self-Compassion:** This website provides information about mindful self-compassion and has guided meditations and exercises, information about workshops, training, online courses and books. Dr Chris Germer is a clinical psychologist, author and teacher of mindfulness and compassion in psychotherapy. He also co-developed the Mindful Self-Compassion training programme with Dr Kristin Neff. **ChrisGermer.com** and **www.mindfulselfcompassion.org**

- **Centre for Mindful Self-Compassion:** This website is about self-compassion, it offers guided meditations and exercises, and has tips on how to practice. It also has information about courses, an online practice group and a good resource list. **www.centerformsc.org**

- **Self-Compassion:** This website provides information about self-compassion, has a self-compassion test, offers guided meditations and

exercises, has tips on how to practice, information about workshops / training and offers a good resource list. Dr Kristin Neff is an international expert on self-compassion, a researcher, author and the co-developer of the Mindful Self-Compassion training programme.
www.self-compassion.org

* **The Compassionate Mind Foundation:** The Compassionate Mind Foundation promotes wellbeing and compassion. The website has information about compassion, workshops, guided meditations, books and articles.
www.compassionatemind.co.uk

Websites – Mindfulness

* **Mindful website:** This website is dedicated to inspiring and guiding anyone who wants to explore mindfulness. It provides information for living and for work. It also offers tips on how to meditate and has guided meditation exercises. It also produces a magazine. **www.mindful.org**

* **Centre for Mindfulness Research and Practice:** This is based at Bangor University and the website provides information on courses on mindfulness, as well as teacher training.
www.bangor.ac.uk/mindfulness

* **Mindfulness Association:** The Mindfulness Association website provides information on mindfulness, courses and teacher training. It also has information on research, books, guided meditations, exercises, apps and events. It also has a blog. **www.mindfulnessassociation.net**

* **Breathworks Mindfulness:** This website provides information on mindfulness courses such as, mindfulness in the workplace/mindfulness and health and also online courses. It has information on teacher training, research, retreats and events. It also has a newsletter and a blog. The online shop sells books,

DVDs, CDs and downloadable guided meditations and exercises.
www.breathworks-mindfulness.org.uk

Books

- Brach, T. (2003) *Radical Acceptance: Embracing your life with the heart of a Buddha*, New York: Bantam.
- Brown, B. (1999) *Soul without shame: A guide to liberating yourself from the judge within*, Boston: Shambala.
- Brown, B. (2010) *The Gifts of Imperfection*, Center City, MN: Hazelden.
- Brown, B (2015) *Rising Strong*, Vermilion.
- Germer, C. K. (2009) *The mindful path to self-compassion: Freeing yourself from destructive thoughts and emotions*, New York: Guilford Press.
- Gilbert, P. (2009) *The compassionate mind*, London: Constable.
- Goldstein, J., & Kornfield, J. (1987) *Seeking the heart of wisdom: The path of insight meditation*, Boston: Shambhala.
- Hanh, T.N (2011) *Your True Home and the everyday wisdom of Thich Naht Hanh*, Boston: Shambala.
- Hanh T. N. (1997) *Teachings on love*, Berkeley, CA: Parallax Press.
- Hanson, R (2013) *Hardwiring Happiness: The New Brain Science of Contentment, Calm, and Confidence*, Harmony.
- Kabat- Zinn, J (2005) *Wherever you go there you are: Mindfulness Meditation in everyday Life*, Hyperion; 10th revised edition.
- Kornfield, J. (1993) *A path with heart*, New York: Bantam Books.

- **Neff, K (2011)** *Self–compassion. Stop Beating Yourself Up and Leave Insecurity Behind*, **William Morrow & Company.**
- **Salzberg, S. (2005)** *The force of kindness: change your life with love and compassion,* **Boulder, CO: Sounds True.**
- **Seigel, D. (2007)** *Mindfulness and the Brain,* **W.W.Norton & Company.**
- **Sood, A. and Mayo Clinic (2015)** *The Mayo Clinic Handbook for Happiness: A Four-Step Plan for Resilient Living,* **Da Capo Lifelong Books.**
- **Tolle, E. (2005)** *The Power of Now: A guide to Spiritual Enlightenment,* **Yellow Kite.**

Most of the above authors have written other great books on the subject of mindfulness, self-compassion and happiness, so you've got some treats in front of you if you want to read more.

Meditation Apps

- **Insight Timer: Free to download**
  'Insight Timer' has many guided meditations, music and talks for beginners and also for the more experienced. It also offers a social network for meditators with a map showing how many people in the world are meditating at any one time. Friends can also be invited to join in, and discuss topics related to mindfulness in the 'Insight groups'.
- **Smiling Mind: Free to download**
  'Smiling Mind' covers 'What is Mindfulness' and offers programmes for specific age groups. It also gives information for parents who wish to help their children practice mindfulness. It offers a range of programmes, including 'Sport', 'Mindfulness in the Classroom' and 'Mindfulness in the Workplace'.

- **MindFi: Free to download**

  'MindFi' includes meditations for the beginner to the more advanced. These are linked to key points of the day, such as meal times. The app also plays calming sounds.

- **Mindfulness Daily: Free to download**

  'Mindfulness Daily' covers a 21-day programme of short guided practices including 'Mindful Breathing', 'Body Awareness', 'Kindness' and 'Present Moment Awareness'.

- **10% Happier: Free to download with optional monthly subscription**

  '10% Happier' has introductory sessions. Daily videos and guided meditations teach the essentials and go through the practice. There's practical advice for applying mindfulness to such things as relationships, eating and work. There are also quick meditations that fit into busy lives e.g. for commutes and lunch breaks. The monthly subscription fee gives access to new videos and guided meditations.

- **Buddhify: Pay**

  'Buddhify' has a colourful wheel divided into segments, where each segment represents exercises in mindfulness and meditation. Exercises covers things such as 'Walking', 'Work Break', 'Going to Sleep' and 'Waking Up'. Sessions are for both beginners and for those with more experience. These vary in length from 3–40 minutes long.

- **Headspace: Free to download with optional monthly subscription**

  'Headspace' covers the basics of mindfulness and meditation. The free version gives a set number of guided meditations and some 'mini' practices. The monthly subscription fee gives access to more.

- **Stop, Breathe and Think: Free to download with optional monthly subscription**

  'Stop, Breathe and Think' starts with a mental and physical 'check in'. The app then recommends short guided meditations, yoga and acupressure videos, best suited to the mood identified. The free version gives about 30 meditation exercises. The monthly subscription gives access to many more exercises.

- **Aura: Free to download with optional monthly subscription**
  'Aura' focuses on short meditations. Sessions change daily and include exercises such as, 'Time alone in Nature' and 'Belly Breathing'. The monthly subscription gives access to many more exercises. The app also has a 'daily reflection' area that allows gratitude to be recorded. Each day feelings are logged and these become a graph that visually tracks daily mood.

- **Calm: Free to download with optional monthly subscription**
  'Calm' offers a range of free meditation exercises, including a beginner's programme. This covers the basics, such as mindful breathing. The guided meditation sessions are available in lengths from 3-25 minutes. The app has programmes for beginners, intermediates and advanced users. It also offers calming music and a selection of 'sleep stories'. The monthly subscription gives access to more meditations.

Ted Talks

The following people (and many others) have presented some great 'Ted Talks':

- Kristin Neff
- Brene Brown
- Sharon Salzberg

These can be accessed via **www.ted.com/talks**

YouTube

- **Tarah Brach**
- **Jack Kornfield**
- **Sharon Salzberg**
- **Kristin Neff**
- **Chris Germer**
- **Brene Brown**

These can be accessed via www.youtube.com

This is the lovely Annabelle, shy and timid…and one of the inspirations for this book.